Vermont Chap Book

Vermont Chap Book

Being

A Garland of Ten Folk Ballads

together with

Notes by Helen Hartness Flanders
Preface by Donald Davidson
Illustrations by Arthur Healy

Granger Index Reprint Series

BOOKS FOR LIBRARIES PRESS
FREEPORT, NEW YORK

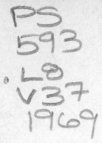
Copyright 1941, The Middlebury College Press,
Middlebury, Vermont
Copyright © 1968, Helen Hartness Flanders
Reprinted 1969 by arrangement
with Helen Hartness Flanders
All rights reserved

STANDARD BOOK NUMBER:
8369-6016-5

LIBRARY OF CONGRESS CATALOG CARD NUMBER:
70-76935

MANUFACTURED
BY
HALLMARK LITHOGRAPHERS, INC.
IN THE U.S.A.

A Garland of Ten Folk Ballads

as they were sometime known to
The People of Vermont
and as they now repose in
The Helen Hartness Flanders Collection
in the Middlebury College Library

Thus like the Miller bold and free
    Let us rejoice and sing;
The days of youth are made for glee,
    And Time is on the wing.
This song shall pass from me to thee
    Along this jovial ring.

From MILLER OF DEE

PREFACE

It seems peculiarly appropriate that the ten ballads included in this volume should be printed from type set by hand in a cabin at Bread Loaf. That cabin looks on a meadow where devil's paint-brush and large upland daisies bloom. The meadow slopes to a brook that flows through woods of spruce and birch. Beyond the brook (and all around) are the Green Mountains of Vermont. Across the road from the cabin are the buildings of the Bread Loaf School of English, among them the original farm-house, inn, and barn of Joseph Battell, the father of Bread Loaf. The members of the printing class are graduate students, most of them English teachers. They come to the printer's rule straight from their very advanced and scholarly courses, and do not find the transition odd. Three miles down the road is Ripton, a village from which Ed Dragon, a ballad singer over eighty years old, will lightsomely issue to raise a song or to dance a tune. Further on, in the valley, is Middlebury College, the *alma mater* of all this. And Middlebury College is the fortunate trustee and keeper of the Helen Hartness Flanders Collection, a remarkable treasury of balladry and folksong of which these ten pieces are a delightful and valuable sample. Mrs. Flanders, herself a Vermont cosmopolite, has travelled the highways and byways of the State for the past eleven years, collecting words and tunes of folk ballads which in another generation would be lost forever.

Thus do things go pleasantly together at Bread Loaf in Vermont. From the higher literary studies to simple things like singing a ballad or setting it in type is only a matter of stepping across the road. In a truly human world, it would be always thus: abstract and particular, book and life, never far apart—but close together, as meadow, print-shop, ballad, college, and scholarly specialties are close together while these lines are being set. The world of our day seems to want it otherwise, but so much the worse for it. Too long we have indulged ourselves recklessly in division and specialization—in the kind of dissociation which, for doubtful practical gains, scatters the parts of our lives, often to great distances. And look at the result: commotions ruinous enough to shake the planet.

When there is not too much distance between the "high" and the "low" parts of a culture, the Homeric poem is born, or *Beowulf*; or, in more immediate tradition, Chaucer, who flourishes alongside ballad and carol. To-day, what a distance there is between the poems of T. S. Eliot and the thing that passes for popular song. Too much refinement on one side and too low a vulgarization on the other—it is an unhealthy condition. This book, if it symbolizes a tendency, may suggest our instinctive recoil from such cultural gaps. Our arts may presently become less refined, our lives less scattered. Our interest in ballads, anticipatory of that healthy change, thus differs greatly from the Nineteenth Century interest, which was antiquarian and romantic, or else scientific.

The ten ballads and folksongs here presented reflect very decidedly an Eighteenth Century context. That was a time in American life when, culturally speaking, it was still easy to step across the road. The ballads will have points of interest to many kinds of readers, including specialists. They will be most completely enjoyed by people who understand the context in which they belong and are aware of the implications of that understanding—people, for example, who, loving Vermont, know that its goodness (like the goodness of other American places rural and mountain) comes largely from having kept its distances short, from having wished not to depart irretrievably from its Eighteenth Century, or original American, foundation. To be wholly alive, of course, these songs must be sung; but the tunes are lost, or were not found by the collector. I am sure that Miss Marguerite Olney, Curator of the Flanders Collection, will be very grateful if any reader who knows the proper tune for a ballad will furnish it. Meanwhile, there are typical ballad tunes that will serve.

A certain "literary" quality invades some of the ballads, notably the sentimental ones, like "The Beckwith Tragedy," "Joel Baker," "The Calais Disaster," "The Indian Student." Relatively modern ballads all reflect a somewhat weakened folk tradition and furthermore do not assimilate the "high" literary tradition as well as did their Fourteenth and Fifteenth Century predecessors. But they do assimilate, to some extent, what the Eighteenth and early Nineteenth Centuries have to offer, and the moral and sentimental defect, if it is a defect, comes from the literary *milieu* rather than from the nature of folksong itself. Even in their awkwardness they are a shade more realistic and genuine than Whittier's admirable "Song of the Vermonters," which has the sentiment but not the idiom of the folk. But Whittier passed into oral tradition, nevertheless.

The other pieces are true native American folksong, locally Vermont and New England in flavor and idiom, even while they carry echoes of a more distant past. The comic wooer of "Jonathan's Courtship," like the greenhorns of "The Hog-Thorny Bear," is the victim of a broad country joke in a very local setting; but both wooer and greenhorns go far back in folk tradition. The "segar-smoker's" reflections on the wars and politics of his day derive some of their calm from the New England temperament, and some, too, I think, from the "philosophical tobacco" of Elizabethan song. The satirical catalogue of "Hard Times" also has its Elizabethan and medieval analogues, but title and detail are American. Some of the texts, I imagine, are unique. "Bill Hopkins' Colt" must surely be. I recall no other ballad about a horse trade. All of the ballads reflect specific frontier experiences even while they fall into conventional patterns. Evidently the ballad makers of Vermont had, as Mr. Eliot so prettily says of John Donne, a sensibility that could devour any experience and a form for handling it. But we do not need to worry over that issue. The main thing, with a good ballad, is to pass it on.

—DONALD DAVIDSON

CONTENTS

Vermont Chap Book

The Song of the Vermonters, 1779

Sometimes the work of a professional poet so stirs the hearts of the people as to be adopted as their own. In 1833, John Greenleaf Whittier, early interested in the history of Vermont and in Ethan Allen, "whose life and adventures awakened the enthusiasm even of a Quaker boy, whose peace principles at that time were traditionary rather than the result of serious convincement," wrote "The Song of the Vermonters" as a literary hoax. "I was curious," he confessed forty-four years later, "to see if it could be received as an old-time production." How well he succeeded is proved by the inclusion of these verses under "Ballad Literature" in the 1856 edition of Duyckinck's "Cyclopedia of American Literature." The editor's note dates the ballad 1779, at the time when New Hampshire, Massachusetts, and New York were hotly contesting their rights to the territory of the present state of Vermont, and Vermonters were as hotly defying them all.

THE SONG OF THE VERMONTERS, 1779

Ho—all to the borders! Vermonters, come down,
With your breeches of deer-skin, and jackets of brown;
With your red woolen caps, and your moccasins, come,
To the gathering summons of trumpet and drum.

Come down with your rifles!—let grey wolf and fox
Howl on in the shade of their primitive rocks;
Let the bear feed securely from pig-pen and stall;
Here's a two-legged game for your powder and ball.

On our South come the Dutchmen, enveloped in grease;
And, arming for battle, while canting of peace;
On our East, crafty Meshech has gathered his band
To hang up our leaders, and eat out our land.

Ho—all to the rescue! For Satan shall work
No gain for his legions of Hampshire and York!
They claim our possessions,—the pitiful knaves,—
The tribute *we* pay, shall be prisons and graves!

Let Clinton and Ten Broek, with bribes in their hands,
Still seek to divide us, and parcel our lands;—
We've coats for our traitors, whoever they are;
The warp is of *feathers*—the filling of *tar*!

Does the "old Bay State" threaten? Does Congress complain?
Swarms Hampshire in arms on our borders again?
Bark the war-dogs of Britain aloud on the lake?
Let 'em come;—what they *can*, they are welcome to take.

What seek they among us? The pride of our wealth
Is comfort, contentment, and labour and health,
And lands which, as Freemen, we only have trod,
Independent of all, save the mercies of God.

Yet we owe no allegiance; we bow to no throne;
Our ruler is law, and the law is our own;
Our leaders themselves are our own fellow-men,
Who can handle the sword, or the scythe, or the pen.

Our wives are all true, and our daughters are fair,
With their blue eyes of smiles, and their light flowing hair;
All brisk at their wheels till the dark even-fall,
Then blithe at the sleigh-ride, the husking, and ball!

We've sheep on the hill sides; we've cows on the plain;
And gay-tasseled corn-fields, and rank-growing grain;
There are deer on the mountains; and wood-pigeons fly
From the crack of our muskets, like clouds on the sky.

And there's fish in our streamlets and rivers, which take
Their course from the hills to our broad-bosomed lake;
Through rock-arched Winooski the salmon leaps free,
And the portly shad follows all fresh from the sea.

4

Like a sun-beam the pickerel glides through his pool;
And the spotted trout sleeps where the water is cool;
Or darts from his shelter of rock and of root
At the beaver's quick plunge, or the angler's pursuit.

And ours are the mountains, which awfully rise
'Till they rest their green heads on the blue of the skies;
And ours are the forests unwasted, unshorn,
Save where the wild path of the tempest is torn.

And though savage and wild be this climate of ours,
And brief be our season of fruits and of flowers,
Far dearer the blast round our mountains which raves,
Than the sweet summer zephyr, which breathes over slaves.

Hurra for VERMONT! for the land which we till
Must have sons to defend her from valley and hill;
Leave the harvest to rot on the field where it grows,
And the reaping of wheat for the reaping of foes.

From far Michiscoui's wild valley, to where
Poosoomsuck steals down from his wood-circled lair,
From Shocticook river to Lutterlock town,—
Ho—all to the rescue! Vermonters, come down.

Come York or come Hampshire,—come traitors and knaves
If ye rule o'er our *land*, ye shall rule o'er our *graves*;
Our vow is recorded—our banner unfurled;
In the name of Vermont we defy *all the world!*

5

The Indian Student

These verses are included in a manuscript blankbook of songs current at the time of the American Revolution, successively the property of Edmund and Joseph Grandy of Panton, Vermont, and now in the Harris Collection at Brown University. Mr. Charles E. Tuttle of Rutland, Vermont, loaned the book to the Flanders Collection for copying. Another Indian student, appearing in folk song tradition shortly after 1812, was "Young Strongbow" of Dartmouth College.

THE INDIAN STUDENT

On susquehannahs untmos spring
Where savage tribes pursue their game
With blanket tired with yellow strings
The Shepherd of the forest came

Not long before a wandering priest
His wish exprest with visage sad
Ah! why he cry'd in satans waste
Ah, why detain so fine a lad

In Yankee land their stands a town
Where learning may be purchas'd low
Exchange his blanket for a gown
And let the lad to College go

From long debate the council rose
And viewing Shalmes tricks with Joy
To Harvard hall Oer drifted Snow
They sent the tauney coloured boy

A while he read a while he wrote
A while he studied grammers rules
An Indian savage so well bred
Great credit promised to the schools

7

Some thought in law he would excell
Some thought in physic he would shine
And some who lik'd him passing well
Beheld in him the sound Divine

But some with more deserning eye
Could even then new phrases shew
They saw him lay his Virgil by
To wander with his dearer bow

The tedious hour of studdy spent
The heavy moulded lecture don
He to the woods a hunting went
But sighed to see the setting sun

The shady banks the purling stream
The woody wiles his heart possest
The dewy lawns his morning dream
In Nature's fairest fancy drest

Ah why he Cry'd did I forsake
My native shades for gloomy walls
The silver streams the limpid lakes
For musty Books and College halls

A little Could my wants supply
Can wealth or Honor give me more
Or will the Silvan gods deny
The Humble treat he gave before

Where natures ancient forest grows
And mingled laurel never fades
My heart is fixt and I must go
To die among my native Shades

He spake & to the western Springs
His gown exchang'd his money spent
His blanket tie'd with yellow strings
The Shepherd of the forest went

Returning to his native plain
The Indians welcomed him with Joy
The council took him home again
And blest the tawny coloured boy

Beckwith Tragedy

Dr. Beauchamp wrote, in 1899, in the "Journal of American Folklore," Volume XII: "On my return home a friend had rescued another ballad for me, written on time-discolored paper, with an antique British water-mark, being evidently the ballad in the hand-writing of its author. It is entitled 'A short account of the awful and surprising death of the child of Daniel Beckwith, who departed this life June ye 20th day, A. D. 1773.'" This ballad has all the characteristics of early American folk-expression, and the place-names suggest a Vermont origin.

BECKWITH TRAGEDY

my frends allow my febel toungue,
if I may speak my mind,
this plainly shoes to old and young
the frailty of mankind.

the child that in the woods retiar
is lost while parants moarn,
and others are consumd by fiar
or into peses toarn.

permit my febel pen to rite
what has been laitly dun,
a man who plast his cheaf delight
in his beloved son.

in manchester whare he ingoys
provision for this life,
he had two dafters and three boys
by his beloved wife.

his second son, robbens by name,
was ten years old and moar,
on him this sad distruction came,
who was in peses toar.

the father said, "my children thair
if you will clear sum land,
you shall posses all it doth bair
to be at your command."

the parants then did both agree,
to tinmouth took their way,
a moarning sister for to see
but long they did not stay.

the prity boys, we understand,
did lovingly agree
all for to clear the peas of land
set fiar to a tree.

the chunk was thirty feet in length
and was exceding dry,
so rotten it had not much strength
did burn most vemantly.

the boys against a log did lean
or on it setting all,
and nothing was for to be seen
until the tree did fall.

but, Oh, alass, the dismall blow
struck robbens to the ground,
his head was masht two peses soo,
a deep and deadly wound.

his head and arms all broke to bits,
he in the fiar did lye,
the children scard out of their wits
aloud began two cry.

the elder son that yet remains,
resevd a grevous wound,
but, Oh, alass, poor robbens brains
did fall out on the ground.

thus he within the flame did lye,
the others full of greaf,
a neighbor that did hear them cry
did run to their releaf.

this maid his tender heart to ake
to see him in that case;
he quickly hold on him did take
and drue him from that place.

now near the middel of the day
the neighbors thay did meat,
the corps they quickly did convay
in to his winding sheat.

a frend to tinmouth took his coast
the hevey news to beair.
the tidings come to them all most
as soon as thay got their.

13

but when the parants come two know
theair son was dead indeed,
alass, their eys with tears did flow
and homwards went with spead.

the peopel came from every part
to see the awfull sight,
it grevd the parants tendar hart,
alass, and well it might.

to see their one beloved son
in such a case indeed,
me thinks would make a hart of stone
or hart of steall to blead.

laid in the grave two turn to dust,
their greaf what tongue can tell,
but yet, alass, the parants must
bid him a long fair well.

THE SARTINTY OF DETH

see, the vain race of mortal man
are but an empty show,
like bubbles on the water stan
and seen two nothing goo.

when wee are well, alass, our breth
is easy took away,
ten thousand ways a mortal deth
can turn our flesh to clay.

the old and young, both high and low,
must yeald their mortal breth,
when is the time we doe not know,
but all must suffer deth.

to conker deth, if we contrive,
it is in vain to try,
for suarly as wee are alive,
soo suarly wee must die.

FINIS

November ye 20, 1773

Jonathan's Courtship

The sons of Mary Bartlett Eaton, a native of Sutton, Vermont, remember her singing about this amusing courtship nearly seventy years ago. The words were furnished by Mr. H. S. Eaton of Westfield, Massachusetts. They differ slightly from the broadside possessed by the late Mrs. Ella Doten of North Calais, Vermont. Both contain graphic colloquial idioms.

JONATHAN'S COURTSHIP

A merry tale I will rehearse
As ever you did hear,
How Jonathan set out so fine
To see his dearest dear.

His father gave him a new suit
When he was one and twenty,
Besides a prancing nag to boot
And money, sir, in plenty.

And, more than that, I'd have you know
That he had got some knowledge,
Enough for common use or so,
But never'd been to college.

A hundred he could count, 'tis said,
And in the Bible read,
And by good Christian parents bred
Could almost say the creed.

One day his mother said to him,
"Come here, my son, come here.
Go dress you up so neat and trim
And go a-courtin, dear."

"What in the plague does mother want?
 I snigs I das'n't go marm,
 I shall get funned, and then plague on't,
 Folks'll laugh at me so, marm."

"Poh Poh, fix up, and you shall go
 To see the deacon's Sary,
 She has a large estate you know,
 Besides she wants to marry.

"She has chintz gowns and ribbins fine
 And all things her befittin,'
 A cow, two sheep, pig, cat, cock hen,
 And pad to ride to meetin.

"Now Jonathan, I bid ye go,
 Ye'll never git more money,
 And I will make a weddin cake
 Almost as sweet as honey."

So Jonathan in best array
Did mount his dappled nag,
Tho he trembled sadly all the way
Lest he should get the bag.

When he got there, as people say,
Twas nearly six o'clock:
And Moll cried out "Come in, I say."
As soon as he did knock.

He made twixt two and three great bows,
Just as his mother taught him,
The which were droll enough to see,
You'd think the cramp had caught him.

At length came in the deacon's Sal
From milking at the barn.
She was as plump a looking gal
As ever twisted yarn.

All ladies now, as I would guess,
And many a lady's man,
Would like to know about her dress.
I'll tell you what I can.

Her wrapper, grey, was not so bad.
Her apron, it was blue.
A stocking on one foot she had,
And on the other foot a shoe.

Now Jonathan, he scratched his head
When first he saw his dear,
Got up, sat down, and nothing said
Because he felt so queer.

But soon the folks went off to bed,
It seemed they took the hint,
While Jonathan was some afraid,
Sal tho't the old cat was in't.

The Segar

"The Segar" appeared as a broadside around 1827-1829, printed by Ashbel Stoddard of Hudson, N. Y. Mr. Charles E. Tuttle of Rutland, Vermont, made the broadside available to the Flanders Collection. Assumedly, these ruminations would end as the author lights another segar if they were in a leisurely tune—but we do not know the tune.

THE SEGAR

The old year is gone, and a new one begun,
I'll set by the fire by my wife and my son;
While others are playing destruction and war,
I'll set by the fire and smoke my Segar.

Although winter rageth, I'll laugh at the storm,
My great coat around me will keep me quite warm;
All sorrows and troubles I'll drive them afar,
I'll set by the fire and smoke my Segar.

Let the tide of opinion before England or France,
I'll set at my ease till I see it advance,
Let wheat be high prized or corn above par,
I'll set by the fire and smoke my Segar.

Let Justice and Juryman do Justice on the throne,
Let Federals or Republicans make good laws or none,
Let Sheriffs and let Constables stand forty on the square,
I care not for either, I'll smoke my Segar.

In opinions I will never fall out with a friend,
My secrets I never will reveal unto men;
And when I am call'd to the war,
I'll send out another and smoke my Segar.

When my Segar falls to ashes another I'll take,
But when man falls, he falls never to awake.
Like life's fleeting moments I'll never complain,
How soon it extinguish is just like a flame.

Bill Hopkins' Colt

Many a song in Vermont pokes fun in a popular tune at some local event that people like to sing as well as talk about. Horse racing crops up in different songs. Up in the Connecticut Lakes region, for instance, lines like these are still bandied about in a bantering tune:

> D'ye ever see Winona
> A-comin' down the street
> With clatter of her feet?
> You'd know she'd always get beat.
> Did you ever see Winona when she beat?

And like as not from the opposite side of the street would come
> You'd know she always could be beat.

"Bill Hopkins' Colt" was recorded by Mr. George Brown in 1930 in Grafton, Vermont, as remembered by Mr. George Howe. It was from Mr. Herbert Day, brother-in-law to Mr. Howe, that we secured the complete text. It is sung to a variant of "Solomon Levi."

BILL HOPKINS' COLT

Twas over in Cambridge county
In a barroom filled with smoke,
Where the nabobs gather in at night,
Talk horse and crack a joke.

Twas on a blustering winter's night
With tongues all ready greased,
And smoke rolled from his old clay pipe
When Bill Hopkins spoke his piece.

I'd like to tell you, boys, about the colt
My Dad was going to shoot,
Yes, he was going to take a life,
The crooked-legged brute.

He was so tarnal mad, you see,
To think old dollar mare
Would mother such a hambletonian
As we saw sprawling there.

But I begged so hard of him
To give the homely thing to me,
At last he says, "Well, take him, Bill,
He's the worst I ever see."

Well, I got him through to four year old,
Though I wouldn't have owned it,
I'd have swapped him for a mule
If no one would have knowned it.

For it's long-legged and slab-sided
Was the make up of the creature,
And the boys all laughed at me,
So I kept him down in the back lot
Well out of sight, you see.

There I'd go and stir him up
And switch him round the lot
To see if he couldn't strike a gait
That looked to me like a trot.

He didn't seem to have a gait,
But mixed himself all up
Like an old jackknife with rivets loose,
Half open and half shut.

I broke him and I drove him
But he didn't seem to know
If drove single or drove double
How he'd ought to act or go.

I hauled milk to the factory
With him and our old mare,
And one night while coming home
I found out what was there.

The pole slipped through the neck yoke ring
While coming down the hill,
And they let out, Jehosaphat!
They let out for to kill.

My surprise turned to amazement,
My blood got biling hot,
For the old mare ran her level best
But the colt just kept his trot.

Well, going up the hill
I fixed things up all right,
I told my secret to no one
Nor slept myself that night.

For the county fair was coming off
And I'd made up my mind,
I'd stand a chance with four year olds
And not get far behind.

So I got a chap to enter him
So no one else would know
What colt was going to trot, my boys,
Till called up for to go.

We scored and scored to get the word,
My colt would sprawl and skip
And the boys would laugh and holler,
"Bill, why don't you let him rip?"

At last we got the word to go
And the others were far ahead,
I wished that I was somewhere else
And the darned old colt was dead.

I hauled right up and pounded him
The very best I knew,
And all at once
He spread himself and flew,

Well, talk about your trotting, boys,
And talk about your fun,
Twas when I downed those four year olds,
And I downed them one by one.

My colt won three straight heats,
The crowd went crazy wild,
To see that ere colt win
Like taking candy from a child.

Well, boys, to close my story,
You know the place I own?
Well, the price I got for that colt
Just deeded me that home.

Now, my old man thinks
That blooded stock is his best holt,
But you bet your life he never gives away
Another crooked-legged colt.

Joel Baker

A valuable collector's item is a booklet entitled "The Green
Mountain Songster, Being a Collection of Songs on Various
Subjects. Principally tending to expel melancholy and cheer
the drooping mind." It contains many songs, old in oral tradition when printed at Sandgate, Vermont, in 1823 "by an
ex-revolutionary soldier." The only known copy, owned by
Mr. Harold Rugg of the Baker Memorial Library at Hanover, N. H., includes "Joel Baker," whose untimely end must
have been noised across the mountains in southern Vermont,
still savoring of the pulpit and the tombstone.

JOEL BAKER

Come all young lovers far and near,
A dismal story you shall hear,
A young man did in Alstead dwell
Who lov'd a fair maid passing well.

To her he went with tears 'tis said,
And many solemn vows they made;
She, false girl, fill'd his heart with wo,
Which sent him to the shades below.

And when so cruel she did prove,
And thus her true love did abuse,
By choosing of another one
He cried I'm utterly undone.

To her he went and thus he cried,
Dear Sally, will you be my bride?
For sure our vows must end the strife
Or cut the brittle thread of life.

No answer from her could he gain
To ease him from his bitter pain;
He said you've pierc'd my tender heart,
Alas, this world and I must part!

Now when her parents this did hear,
They said we fear his death draws near.
With scornfulness the damsel spoke—
I soon will send him to a rope.

'Twas on July, the second day,
Oh, when the sun had roll'd away;
Then by a musket's dismal sound,
His body by some friends was found.

His body did lay on the floor,
And from it ran the purple gore;
Three deadly groans he gave, 'tis true,
Then bid this sinful world adieu.

'Tis said the young man he was poor,
'Tis true, he had no great in store;
I think I hear that fame does say,
What the other gains is by the way.

Now her new will I shall not name,
Although he says there's none to blame;
Oh, from my heart I wish them well,
For none but God alone can tell.

Scarce had a month then pass'd away,
When she with her new love did stay;
Much would they dread and greatly fear,
Then should his frightful ghost appear.

32

Now lovers all, I pray be true,
Don't break your vows, what ere you do:
The God above rules all below,
May punish you with nameless wo.

Some passed by his grave, 'tis said,
And there cast slurs upon the dead;
The time will come and soon will be,
They must lie there as well as he.

Now to conclude and make an end;
I sat me down—these lines I've pen'd—
God grant it may a warning be,
To all who do these verses see.

The Hog-Thorny Bear

Songs made up by early New Englanders seldom recount a public "come-uppance" or practical joke. Here is an exception which, to judge by its refrain, must have been set to an Irish air. Miss Constance Upham, now of Springfield, Vermont, heard it as a child, sung by an old man in Windham, as made up by Stephen Streeter in 1820. She cannot recall its tune.

THE HOG-THORNY BEAR

I call the attention of each merry blade.
Be still as a mouse and let nothing be said.
I'll sing you a song it will please you to hear,
How lately two men had a fray with a bear.

> *Chorus:* Musha tuther-a-la
> Tuth-a-la tuther-a-la
> Musha tuther-a-la.

It was one Tabor Coombs and Sam Esterbrooks,
They were not very handsome but quite clever folks.
'Twas on Turkey Mountain, I think it was there,
They had such a terrible fray with a bear.

> *Chorus:*

One evening as they were returning from work,
'Twas through the thick forest so dreary and mirk,
Said one to the other, "I'm not without fear
That ere we reach home we shall meet with a bear."

> *Chorus:*

With these apprehensions and while they were fresh
They heard a loud clambering noise in the brush.
The dog he did bark and erect stood his hair,
And both cried at once, "Behold, there is a bear:"

> *Chorus:*

35

Hard Times

This ballad is copied from the broadside in a scrapbook treasured by the late Mrs. Ella Doten of North Calais, Vermont. The broadside was originally "Sold wholesale and retail, by Leonard Deming, at the Sign of the Barber's Pole, No. 61, Hanover Street, Boston, and at Middlebury, Vermont." Deming was a Middlebury printer of the early nineteenth century; his son owned the barber shop in Boston. Fortunately, some professions contributory to "Hard Times" are now extinct.

HARD TIMES

Well, since you request it, I'll sing you a song,
And tell you how people do jumble along;
But the times are so bad, that we scarcely can live,
So I nothing shall ask, if you've nothing to give,
            In these hard times.

The *Doctor* will dose you with physic and squills,
With blisters and clysters, and powders, and pills;
Till your cash is expended, then breathing a home,
He will cry out, poor man, your time it is come,
            But it is hard times.

The *Clothier* will cry out his dye-stuff is scarce,
And as for bank bills, they are all but a farce;
So he must have silver for all that is due,
Yet logwood, soap and vinegar, make a good blue,
            In these hard times.

The *Tailor* will cry out, your pattern is small,
But he may get you a garment by saving it all;
Your silk, your twist, your thread and your lining,
He'll cabbage one half, then charge you for trimming,
            In these hard times.

The *Priest* he will tell you which way you must steer
To save your poor souls, which he holdeth so dear;
But if he don't draw something out of your purse,
He will take off his blessing and whack on a curse,
          In these hard times.

The *Lawyer* will tell you your case it is clear,
If you've plenty of cash you have nothing to fear;
But his fees by bar rules he certainly squares,
And then there's left nothing at all for your heirs,
          In these hard times.

The *Merchant* on goods must have fifty percent,
And as much crave on old debts, and cash that is lent;
But still he has luxuries plenty on hand,
Which he'll coax you to buy, then grapple your land,
          In these hard times.

The *Miller* declares he will grind for your toll,
And do your work well as he can for his soul;
But if you turn your back, with his dish in his fist,
He will leave you the toll, and himself take the grist,
          In these hard times.

The *Carpenter* will tell you he'll build you a house,
So tight and so snug, it won't harbor a mouse,
For two dollars a day, but he won't take a job,
Though he and his apprentice won't half earn their grog,
          In these hard times.

The *Blacksmith* will cry out, his stock is so dear,
He cannot trust out his work but a year;
He'll set a few shoes, or mend your old plough,
And by the next fall he must have your best cow,
          For 'tis hard times.

The *Tanner*, he snatches at every hide
Of your sheep, and your cattle, and horses you ride;
And by the next winter they're lost or proved rotten,
And all that's not marked are surely forgotten,
          In these hard times.

The *Shoemaker* whistles, and hammers, and sweats,
And promises work to pay off his old debts;
You shall have it next week, if existence is spared,
But when the time comes, he is never prepared.
          For 'tis hard times.

The *Pedler* declares that his goods are the best
That ever were brought from the East or the West;
That tin-ware and jewelry, hair-combs and clocks,
Are quite necessary for all clever folks,
          In these hard times.

The *Jeweller* works in the finest of gold,
And makes the best ear-rings that ever were sold;
Tells his pedlers to lie, to dispel ladies' fears,
Till canker and verdigris eat off their ears,
          In these hard times.

The *School-master* pages for want of more pay,
And declares he will have it, or else go away;
Ninety days in each quarter he is strutting about,
Though four weeks make a month, leaving Saturday out,
 In these hard times.

The *Tinker*, he'll tell you he'll mend all your ware,
For little or nothing, but cider and beer,
But in a small patch he'll put nails a full score,
And in stopping one hole he makes twenty more,
 In these hard times.

The *Barber* declares he don't labor for pelf,
Only shaves every blockhead that can't shave himself;
But six cents he must have, from his friends or his foes,
Or else, a bold knave, he won't let go your nose,
 In these hard times.

The *Saddler*, so honest, declares he can't cheat,
With his narrow wool web, and his sheepskin for seat;
A little bog hay for to stuff out the pads,
And must have twenty dollars of our country lads,
 In these hard times.

The old *Farmer* declares he has nothing to spare,
And wishes that Congress would give him a share
Of the surplus cash, to fill up his purse,
And he'd swear he is poor, or any thing worse,
 In these hard times.

The *Hatter* will tell you he'll make you a hat,
From the fleece of a sheep, or a skunk, or a cat;
But he'll take out the fur, and jam in the wool,
And much more he will do, his neighbor to fool,
   In these hard times.

The *Baker* he bakes all the bread that we eat,
And likewise the *Butcher* kills all our fat meat;
They'll hang on the steelyards and make them bear down
And swear there's good weight, when it lacks half a pound,
   In these hard times.

The *Fiddler* will tell you he'll play such a night,
For four dollars he'll play, till it's broad day light;
But before two o'clock, he is sleepy and dull.
He'll take some more grog then he can't play at all,
   In these hard times.

Then there is the *Sheriff*, I almost forgot,
And he is the worst bird we have in our flock;
He will go to your house and take what he please,
And when he's got all, he will double his fees,
   O! then, 'tis hard times.

The *Weaver* he'll tell you he's good at his trade,
If you will fetch your yarn, good cloths shall be made;
But if you watch closely this lover of pelf,
He's pilfering yarn all the time for himself,
   In these hard times.

The *Hunter* for games, searches mountains and hills,
Every thing that he meets he immediately kills;
To wind up the mischief, the good man, perhaps,
Hooks a coon, or a fox, from another man's traps,
        In these hard times.

The *Cooper*, he warrants his work to be nice,
It never will fail, if you keep it from ice;
Full twelve months, or longer, I'll wait for the pay,
The work tumbles down, you are sued by the way,
        In these hard times.

The *Printer* he'll tell you, "Friend, now is the time
To hear from Old England, or some distant clime."
Believe me, poor man, he's your money in view,
Perhaps, when too late, you will find my words true,
        In these hard times.

The *Sailor*, when finding a storm drawing near,
Will lift up his hands to his Maker in fear;
But soon as a calm, he's forgetful of death,
And pours impious curses at every breath,
        In these hard times.

The *Ostler* will give your horse plenty of hay,
And when your back's turn'd, he'll take it away;
For oats he puts chaff, and in corn mixes bran,
And still he cries out, I'm too honest a man,
        In these hard times.

The *Tavern-keeper* and his wife, both will scold,
And call me a villain, perhaps, I'm so bold;
But hand me a drop, just to moisten my clay,
And I'll certainly stop, and no more will I say,
      About hard times.

The Calais Disaster

We have many instances of apt folk-choice in wording and tunes, the result of overwhelming community disasters. Mrs. Ella Doten of North Calais gave the following text, "written by Reuben Waters" after five out of eighteen persons were drowned when their boat sprang a leak on Calais Pond. It seems to be patterned after a song of British tradition, known to Mrs. George Tatro, formerly of Berkshire, Vermont. Her second verse ran:

> Oh Mulberry trembled at that awful stroke;
> Consider the voice of Jehovah that spoke.
> To teach us we are mortal, and exposed to death;
> And subject each moment to yield up our breath.

THE CALAIS DISASTER

Now all you good people of every degree,
Come listen one moment with attention to me.
A sorrowful story I'm going to relate
Of a fatal disaster that happened of late.

O, Calais did tremble at this awful stroke
And considered the voice of Jehovah had spoke
To teach us we're mortals, exposed to death
And subject each moment to yield up our breath.

On Sunday, the fifteenth of June, all so clear,
In the year '73, as many do hear,
A number assembled at Number Ten shore
And went with their boat to Birch Point all o'er.

Their conference being closed, and excursions led away,
All hands for their homes were making straightway;
Down into their boat all hands did repair
And for their homes prepared to steer.

But mark their hard fortune, O mournful, indeed.
Yet no one can hinder what God hath decreed.
The council of Heaven on that fatal day,
By death, in an instant, called numbers away.

A number of people in their health and prime
Called out of the world in an instant of time.
Their boat overturned, plunged them all in the deep
And five out of thirteen, in death fell asleep.

These sorrowful tidings were conveyed straightway
To their friends and relatives without more delay.
But O, their lamenting, no tongue can express,
Or point out their sorrow, great grief and distress.

Seven children bereaved, in their sorrow to mourn
The loss of their parents, no more to return.
Beside Aleck Toby, and his loving wife
Are mourning the loss of a daughter for life.

O, Fayette Teachout, daughter and wife
All were victims in this tragic strife,
Besides Anna Toby and Widdow McKnight,
All were fatal in that tragic flight.

Now all you are living, know you must die.
I pray you take warning by this tragedy
That when death it shall call you and close up your eyes
Your souls may be happy with Christ in the skies.